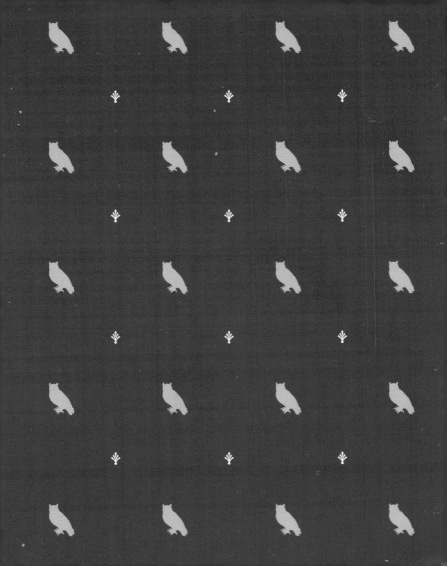

LITTLE BOOK
❦ OF ❦
OWLS

WEIDENFELD & NICOLSON
LONDON

EAGLE OWL AND CAT
WITH DEAD RATS
Johann Heinrich Roos 1631–1685

THE BARN OWL

*W*hite moonlight silvering all the walls,
Through every mouldering crevice falls,
Tipping with white his powdery plume,
As shades or shifts the changing gloom;
The Owl that, watching in the barn,
Sees the mouse creeping in the corn,
Sits still and shuts his round blue eyes
As if he slept – until he spies
The little beast within his stretch –
Then starts – and seizes on the wretch!

THE BARN OWL
Samuel Butler 1612–1680

The Song of the Owl

'I am an owl of orders gray,
  As happy as can be;
The sunny day I dream away
  Within a hollow tree.
But when night comes, with much ado
  I through the forest flit,
    Till on some root
    I rest and hoot –
Tu-woo, tu-woo, tu-woo, tu-woo!
  Tu-whit, tu-whit, tu-whit!

'Unto the minster oft I fly,
  Where, in my ashen cowl,
I hear the winds of summer sigh,
  The winds of winter howl;
Where blue doves woo and bill and coo,
  I on the rafter sit,
    And moping sing
    Beneath my wing,
Tu-woo, tu-woo, tu-woo, tu-woo!
  Tu-whit, tu-whit, tu-whit!'

THE SONG OF THE OWL
R. K. Munkittrick 1853–1911

TAWNY OWL

Maddalena Bouchard 1775

O W L   O N   A   M A G N O L I A   B R A N C H

Kubo Shunman 1757–1820

OWLS

The Wise Owl

There was an owl that lived in an oak,
The more he heard, the less he spoke;
The less he spoke, the more he heard,
O, if men were all like that wise bird!

PUNCH

1875

LITTLE OWLS

———— ⟩⟨ ————

There was an Old Man of Dumbree
Who taught little owls to drink tea;
  For he said, 'To eat mice
  Is not proper or nice,'
That amiable Man of Dumbree.

Edward Lear 1812–1888

OWLS

LITTLE OWL

Albrecht Dürer 1471–1528

Tuwhit Tuwhoo

*T*hy tuwhits are lull'd I wot,
    Thy tuwhoos of yesternight,
Which upon the dark afloat,
    So took echo with delight,
    So took echo with delight,
        That her voice untuneful grown,
        Wears all day a fainter tone.

I would mock thy chant anew;
    But I cannot mimick it;
Not a whit of thy tuwhoo.
    Thee to woo to thy tuwhit,
    Thee to woo to thy tuwhit,
        With a lenthen'd loud halloo.
        Tuwhoo, tuwhit, tuwhit, tuwhoo-o-o.

SECOND SONG TO THE OWL
Alfred, Lord Tennyson 1809–1892

AN ASSEMBLY OF BIRDS

Peter Pallion mid-18th century

THE SPECTRAL OWL

*I*n the hollow tree, in the old grey tower,
 The Spectral Owl doth dwell;
Dull, hated, despised, in the sunshine hour,
 But at dusk – he's abroad and well!…
O, when the night falls, and roosts the fowl,
Then, then, is the reign of the Hornèd Owl!

THE OWL

Bryan Waller Procter 1787–1874

A HORNED OWL

Bruno Liljefors 1860–1939

O W L

A . Weisberger c.1900

OWLS

THE SCREECH-OWL

The screech-owl, with ill-boding cry,
  Portends strange things, old women say;
Stops every fool that passes by,
  And frights the school-boy from his play.

THE POLITICIANS

Lady Mary Wortley Montagu 1689–1762

OWLS

THE GREAT BROWN OWL

A GATHERING OF BIRDS MOBBING AN OWL BEFORE A PALACE

Marcello Provenzale 1575 1639

The brown owl sits in the ivy bush,
　And she looketh wondrous wise,
With a horny beak beneath her cowl,
　And a pair of large round eyes.

She sat all day on the selfsame spray,
　From sunrise until sunset;
And the dim, grey light it was all too bright
　For the owl to see in yet.

'Jenny Owlet, Jenny Owlet,' said a merry little bird,
　'They say you're wondrous wise;
But I don't think you see, though you're looking at *me*
　With your large, round, shining eyes.'

But night came soon, and the pale white moon
　Rolled high up in the skies;
And the great brown owl flew away in her cowl,
　With her large, round, shining eyes.

THE GREAT BROWN OWL

Aunt Effie (Jane Euphemia Browne 1811–1898)

SNOWY OWL

John James Audubon 1785–1851

O W L S

THE OWLET

The Owlet leaves her hiding place at noon
And flaps her grey wings in the doubting light
The hoarse jay screams to see her out so soon
And small birds chirp and startle with affright
Much doth it scare the superstitious wight
Who dreams of sorry luck and sore dismay
While cow boys think the day a dream of night
And oft grow fearful on their lonly way
Who fancy ghosts may wake and leave their
    graves by day.

from NOVEMBER
John Clare 1793–1864

GRAVE CREATURE

——————— • ———————

*T*he leaves that rustled on the oak-crowned hill,
And sky that danced among those leaves, are still;
Rest smooths the way for sleep; in field and bower
Soft shades and dews have shed their blended power
On drooping eyelid and the closing flower;
Sound is there none at which the faintest heart
Might leap, the weakest nerve of superstition start;
Save when the Owlet's unexpected scream
Pierces the ethereal vault; and ('mid the gleam
Of insubstantial imagery, the dream,
From the hushed vale's realities, transferred
To the still lake) the imaginative Bird
Seems, 'mid inverted mountains, not unheard.

*G*rave Creature! – whether, while the moon shines bright
On thy wings opened wide for smoothest flight,
Thou art discovered in a roofless tower,
Rising from what may once have been a lady's bower;
Or spied where thou sitt'st moping in the mew
At the dim centre of a churchyard yew;
Or from a rifted crag or ivy tod
Deep in a forest, thy secure abode,
Thou giv'st, for pastime's sake, by shriek or shout,
A puzzling notice of thy whereabout –
May the night never come, nor day be seen,
When I shall scorn thy voice or mock thy mien!

William Wordsworth 1770–1850

HECATE *William Blake* 1757–1827

To the Owl

SHORT-EARED OWL

from The Royal Natural History 1896

*S*ad bird of night, what sorrow calls thee forth,
To vent thy plaints thus in the midnight hour?
Is it some blast that gather in the north,
Threatening to nip the verdure of thy bower?

Is it, sad owl, that Autumn strips the shade,
And leaves thee here, unsheltered and forlorn?
Or fear that Winter will thy nest invade?
Or friendless melancholy bids thee mourn?

O W L S

Shut out, lone bird, from all the feathered train,
To tell thy sorrows to the unheeding gloom;
No friend to pity when thou dost complain,
Grief all thy thought, and solitude thy home.

Sing on, sad mourner! I will bless thy strain,
And pleased in sorrow listen to thy song;
Sing on, sad mourner! to the night complain,
While the lone echo wafts thy notes along.

Is beauty less when down the glowing cheek
Sad, piteous tears in native sorrows fall?
Less kind the heart when anguish bids it break?
Less happy he who lists to pity's call?

Ah no, sad owl! nor is thy voice less sweet
That sadness tunes it, and grief is there;
That Spring's gay notes, unskilled, thou canst repeat;
That sorrow bids thee to the gloom repair.

TO THE OWL
Robert Burns 1759–1796

THE AZIOLA

'Do you not hear the Aziola cry?
  Methinks she must be nigh,'
Said Mary, as we sate
  In dusk, ere the stars were lit, or candles brought;
And I, who thought
  This Aziola was some tedious woman,
Asked, 'Who is Aziola?' How elate
  I felt to know that it was nothing human,
No mockery of myself to fear and hate!
  And Mary saw my soul,
And laughed and said, 'Disquiet yourself not,
  'Tis nothing but a little downy owl.'

OWLS

BRAZILIAN OWL

Albert van der Eeckhout c.1637

Sad Aziola! many an eventide
  Thy music I had heard
By wood and stream, meadow and mountain side,
  And fields and marshes wide, –
Such as nor voice, nor lute, nor wind, nor bird,
  The soul ever stirred;
Unlike and far sweeter than them all:
  Sad Aziola! from that moment I
Loved thee and thy sad cry.

THE AZIOLA

Percy Bysshe Shelley 1792–1822

THE OWL
Caspar-David Friedrich 1774–1840

DUSK

><

*L*ovely are the curves of the white owl sweeping
   Wavy in the dusk lit by one lone star.
Lone on the fir-branch, his rattle-note unvaried,
   Brooding o'er the gloom, spins the brown eve-jar.
Darker grows the valley, more and more forgetting:
   So were it with me if forgetting could be willed.
Tell the grassy hollow that holds the bubbling well-spring,
   Tell it to forget the source that keeps it filled.

LOVE IN THE VALLEY
George Meredith 1828–1909

OWLS

The Owl and the Panther

I passed by his garden, and marked, with one eye,
How the Owl and the Panther were sharing a pie:
The Panther took pie-crust, gravy and meat,
While the Owl had the dish as his share of the treat.
When the pie was all finished, the Owl, as a boon,
Was kindly permitted to pocket the spoon.

THE OWL AND THE PANTHER
Lewis Carroll 1832–1898

O W L S

G. F. Speidl 1631

AN OWL WAITS TO CATCH A RAT

from Beasts & Birds

An Owl's Cry

Downhill I came, hungry, and yet not starved;
Cold, yet had heat within me that was proof
Against the North wind; tired, yet so that rest
Had seemed the sweetest thing under a roof.

Then at the inn I had food, fire, and rest,
Knowing how hungry, cold, and tired was I.
All the night was quite barred out except
An owl's cry, a most melancholy cry

Shaken out long and clear upon the heel,
No merry note, nor cause of merriment,
But one telling me plain what I escaped
And others could not, that night as in I went.

And salted was my food, and my repose,
Salted and sobered, too, by the bird's voice
Speaking for all who lay under the stars,
Soldiers and poor, unable to rejoice.

THE OWL

Edward Thomas 1878–1917

ANGRY OWL

When I was in a summer valley,
In a very secret cranny,
I overheard a violent quarrel
Of a nightingale against an owl.
Their fight was fierce and sharp and tough,
Sometimes soft, then loud and rough,
And each against the other swelled,
And all her evil anger boiled,
And each about the other said,
The very worst things that she could,
But most of all, about their singing,
They disagreed with loud haranguing.

THE OWL AND THE NIGHTINGALE
Anonymous

EAGLE OWL

Edward Lear 1812–1888

THE BARN OWL

from Thorburn's British Birds

Solitary Reign

Save that, from yonder ivy-mantled tow'r
  The moping owl does to the moon complain,
Of such as, wandering near her secret bower
  Molest her ancient solitary reign.

ELEGY WRITTEN IN
A COUNTRY CHURCHYARD
Thomas Gray 1716–1771

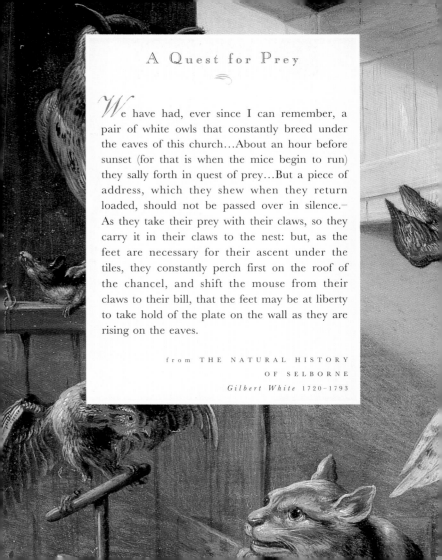

A Quest for Prey

We have had, ever since I can remember, a pair of white owls that constantly breed under the eaves of this church...About an hour before sunset (for that is when the mice begin to run) they sally forth in quest of prey...But a piece of address, which they shew when they return loaded, should not be passed over in silence.– As they take their prey with their claws, so they carry it in their claws to the nest: but, as the feet are necessary for their ascent under the tiles, they constantly perch first on the roof of the chancel, and shift the mouse from their claws to their bill, that the feet may be at liberty to take hold of the plate on the wall as they are rising on the eaves.

from THE NATURAL HISTORY
OF SELBORNE
Gilbert White 1720–1793

A FAMILY OF OWLS,
OTHER BIRDS AND A CAT
Jan van Kessel 1626–1679

LONG-EARED OWL

from Thorburn's British Birds

OWLS

Melancholy's Bird

Come, doleful owl, the messenger of woe,
   Melancholy's bird, compassion of despair,
Sorrow's best friend, and mirth's professèd foe,
   The chief discourser that delights sad care.
O come, poor owl, and tell thy woes to me,
Which having heard, I'll do like for thee.

COME DOLEFUL OWL
Robert Jones fl. 1616

The Fairest Bird

Of all the gay birds that e'er I did see,
The owl is the fairest by far to me,
For all day long she sits on a tree,
And when night comes away flies she.

Anonymous

THE ELEMENTS: AIR
Jan Brueghel 1568–1625

THE HUNGRY LION

Henri Rousseau 1844–1910

THE BOY AND THE OWLS

$$\ast$$

*M*any a time
  At evening, when the earliest stars began
To move along the edges of the hills,
  Rising or setting, would he stand alone,
Beneath the trees, or by the glimmering lake;
  And there, with fingers interwoven, both hands
Pressed closely palm to palm and to his mouth
  Uplifted, he, as though an instrument,
Blew mimic hootings to the silent owls,
  That they might answer him. And they would shout
Across the watery vale, and shout again,
  Responsive to his calls, – with quivering peals,
And long halloos, and screams, and echoes wild
  Redoubled and redoubled; concourse wild
Of mirth and jocund din! And, when there came a pause
  Of silence such as baffled his best skill,
Then, sometimes, in that silence, while he hung
  Listening, a gentle shock of mild surprise
Has carried far into his ear the voice
  Of mountain torrents.

THE BOY AND THE OWLS
William Wordsworth 1770–1850

OWLS

MOUSE FOR SUPPER

*F*ive little owls in an old elm tree,
Fluffy and puffy as owls can be,
Blinking and winking with big round eyes
At the big round moon that hung in the skies:
As I passed beneath, I heard one say,
'There'll be mouse for supper, there will today!'
Then all of them hooted 'Tu-whit, To-whoo!
Yes, mouse for supper, Hoo-hoo, Hoo-hoo!'

TRADITIONAL RHYME

BARN OWLS
Penny Edwin b.1930

CHAT-HUANT   CHOUETTE   HIBOU BRACHYOTE

CHAT-HUANT ÉVEILLÉ   HIBOU SCOPS   HIBOU MOYEN-DUC

LES OISEAUX UTILES À L'AGRICULTURE

from Le Petit Journal 1897

A Silent Night

June 13, 1802. It was a silent night. The stars were out by ones and twos, but no cuckoo, no little birds, the air was not warm…We walked to our new view of Rydale, but it put on a sullen face. There was an owl hooting in Brainriggs. Its first halloo was so like a human shout that I was surprised, when it made its second call tremulous and lengthened out, to find the shout had come from an owl.

Dorothy Wordsworth 1771–1855

OWLS

HER YOUNG ONES

In looks my young do all excel,
Nor nightingales can sing so well.

You'd joy to see the pretty souls
With waddling steps and frowzy polls,
Come creeping from their secret holes.

But I ne'er let them take the air,
The fortune hunters do so stare,
And heiresses indeed they are.

This ancient yew three hundred years,
Has been possess'd by lineal heirs:
The males extinct, now all is theirs.

I hope I've done their beauties right,
Whose eyes out shine the stars by night,
Their muffs and tippets are so white.

THE OWL DESCRIBING HER YOUNG ONES
Anne Finch, Countess of Winchelsea 1666–1720

TAWNY OWLS

Lilian Medland

LES OISEAUX DE
NUIT ET LA LUMIÈRE Nimarr c.1900

OWLS

In the Belfry
❋

*W*hen cats run home and light is come,
And dew is cold upon the ground,
And the far-off stream is dumb,
And the whirring sail goes round,
And the whirring sail goes round;
Alone and warming his five wits,
The white owl in the belfry sits.

*W*hen merry milkmaids click the latch,
And rarely smells the new-mown hay,
And the cock hath sung beneath the thatch
Twice or thrice his roundelay,
Twice or thrice his roundelay;
Alone and warming his five wits,
The white owl in the belfry sits.

SONG – THE OWL
Alfred, Lord Tennyson 1809–1892

THE OWL CRITIC

S N O W Y   O W L
Cecil Gwendolyn Trew

'Who stuffed that white owl?' No one spoke in the shop:
The barber was busy, and he couldn't stop;
The customers, waiting their turns, were all reading
The 'Daily', the 'Herald', the 'Post', little heeding
The young man who blurted out such a blunt question;
No one raised a head, or even made a suggestion;
  And the barber went on shaving.

'Don't you see, Mister Brown,'
Cried the youth, with a frown,
'How wrong the whole thing is,
How preposterous each wing is,
How flattened the head is, how jammed
    down the neck is –
In short, the whole owl, what an ignorant wreck't is!
…Mister Brown! Mister Brown!
Do take that bird down,
Or you'll soon be the laughing-stock all over town!'
    And the barber went on shaving.

Just then, with a wink and a sly normal lurch,
The owl, very gravely, got down from his perch,
Walked round, and regarded his fault-finding critic
(Who thought he was stuffed) with glance analytic,
And then fairly hooted, as if he would say:
'Your learning's at fault *this* time, any way;
Don't waste it again on a live bird, I pray.
I'm an owl; you're another. Sir Critic, good-day!'
    And the barber went on shaving.

from THE OWL CRITIC
James Thomas Fields 1817–1881

FALCON AND DOVE

Adolph von Menzel 1815–1905

GOBLINS AND SPECTRES

✳

White owls seem not (but this I am not positive) to hoot at all: all that clamorous hooting appears to me to come from the wood kinds. The white owl does indeed snore and hiss in a tremendous manner; and these menaces well answer the intention of intimidating: for I have known a whole village up in arms on such an occasion, imagining the church-yard to be full of goblins and spectres. White owls also often scream horribly as they fly along; from this screaming probably arose the common people's imaginary species of screech-owl, which they superstitiously think attends the windows of dying persons.

from THE NATURAL HISTORY OF SELBORNE
Gilbert White 1720–1793

Acknowledgements

Copyright © Weidenfeld and Nicolson 1996
First published in Great Britain in 1996 by
George Weidenfeld and Nicolson Ltd
Orion House, 5 Upper St Martin's Lane,
London WC2H 9EA

All rights reserved. No part of this publication
may be reproduced, stored in a retrieval system,
or transmitted in any form or by any means,
electronic, mechanical, photocopying or
otherwise, without the prior permission in
writing of the copyright owners.

British Library Cataloguing in Publication Data.
A catalogue record for this book is available
from the British Library.

Designed and created by
THE BRIDGEWATER BOOK COMPANY
Words chosen by JOANNE JESSOP
Picture research by FELICITY COX *and*
VANESSA FLETCHER
Page make-up by JANE LANAWAY
Printed in Italy

*The publishers wish to thank the following for
the use of pictures:*
ARCHIV FÜR KUNST UND GESCHICHTE,
London: p.25; Nationalgalerie, Berlin p.54;
Sammlung F. Meyer, Basel p.42; Tate Gallery
p.21; Victoria & Albert Museum p.9. BODLEIAN
LIBRARY, Oxford: p.29 (Owls 262.4 FJC, *Album

Amicorum* of G.F. SPEIDL, Bavaria, 1631–3, MS.
AUTOGR.g.3, f.v). BRIDGEMAN ART LIBRARY: back
cover, p.45; Noortman pp.36–7; Pushkin
Museum p.26; Rafael Valls Gallery p.2;
Victoria & Albert Museum p.6.
J.L. CHARMET, Paris: p.46; Bibliothèque des Arts
Décoratifs p.50. E.T. ARCHIVE: Linnean Society
p.33. FINE ART PHOTOGRAPHIC LIBRARY:
pp.16–17, 40–1, 49. MARY EVANS PICTURE
LIBRARY: p.14. SOTHEBY'S TRANSPARENCY
LIBRARY: front cover, title page, pp.10–11,
12–13, 18, 52.

*Every effort has been made to trace all copyright
holders and obtain permissions. The editor and
publishers sincerely apologise for any inadvertent
errors or omissions and will be happy to correct
them in any future edition.*

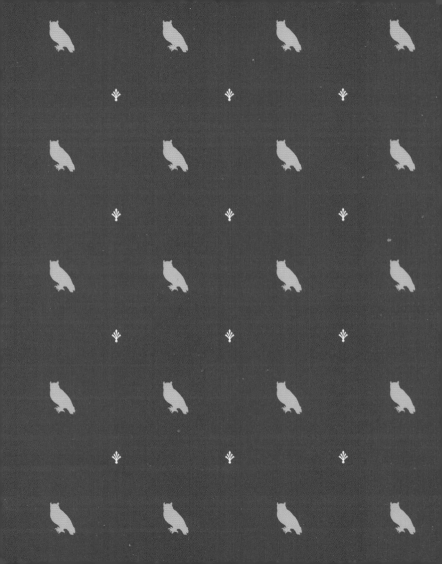